Genre Historical F

MW00588432

Essential Question
Why do people immigrate to new places?

The Promise of Gold Mountain

by Emma Turner ◆ illustrated by Nicole Wong

Chapter 1

From China to Gum San

My name is Wai Ming, and this is the story of why I came to America. I was born in a small village in China. My parents were poor farmers. They worked hard, but their lives were difficult. Sometimes we didn't have enough food to eat.

One day, exciting news reached our village. "Guess what!" my sister said. "Gold has been discovered in a place called California!"

Soon, I began to dream of traveling to Gum San, or Gold Mountain, to make my fortune. If I struck it rich, all my family's problems would be solved! I could see that my parents were worried. But they did not make me stay in China.

It all happened very quickly. Six weeks later, I was on a ship headed for California.

"How old are you?" a man named Mr. Wu asked me.

"Seventeen," I said, trying to look brave.

"That's too young to be alone," Mr. Wu said. "Stay with me. I'll look after you."

The boat trip across the Pacific Ocean took eight weeks. I was seasick the whole time. The ocean was very rough. The food was bad, too! At last, we arrived at San Francisco. Gold fever had hit the city. All the shops were selling pans and shovels. There were 500 empty ships in the harbor. All their crewmen had gone to look for gold!

STOP AND CHECK

Why did Wai Ming leave China?

Chapter 2

At the First Claim

When we got to the camp, the miners were very curious about us. Some inspected our chopsticks. Others pointed to the long braids that hung down our backs or stared at us when we spoke.

"Why are they looking at us?" I whispered to Mr. Wu.

"They've never seen Chinese people before," he said.

Mr. Wu found me a job right away. Every day, I went down to the river. My tools were simple—a pan and a shovel. I filled the pan with sand and gravel from the river. Then I swirled the pan around and looked for bits of gold glittering in the bottom. I worked for 12 hours each day. At night, I slept like a log.

After six months, I grew very homesick.
I even missed my annoying younger sister!
I had to give all the gold I found to the
rich American I worked for. I had to send
all my pay to the man who had paid for my
boat trip to California. I had not saved any
money at all.

Then one night, Mr. Wu came to speak with me. "Good news!" he said. "I can take over a claim the other miners have left. Now, you can work for me!"

STOP AND CHECK

Why was Wai Ming unhappy?

Chapter 3

New Opportunities

About 50 men worked Mr. Wu's claim, a small area where we were allowed to search for gold. We named the place Crows' Creek. We built a dam and a waterwheel to help move water away from the site. This allowed us to dig in the dry streambed for gold. Our system worked like a well-oiled machine.

We worked for long hours, seven days a week. But all our hard work paid off. We began to find gold that we could sell. Finally, I could send money back to my parents. I started to save a little money, too.

Then one day, some American miners arrived at our claim. The men were jealous that we had found gold at an old, abandoned claim.

"California is part of America now," one man said. "We want this gold for ourselves."

The men took over Mr. Wu's claim. There was nothing we could do to stop them. As we got ready to leave, Mr. Wu called me over. "I can't look after you anymore," he said. "Take this, boy. Good luck." Mr. Wu handed me an old jacket. He winked at me, and then he turned and walked away.

STOP AND CHECK

Why did Wai Ming have to leave?

Chapter 4

Alone in America

At that moment, I felt hopeless. I was all alone. I thought of my family in China with nothing. I thought of how easy I had imagined it would all be. What could I do?

Then I remembered Mr. Wu's gift. Why had he given me that jacket? The weather was warm. The jacket wasn't valuable. When I put it on, it felt strangely heavy. There was something hidden in the pocket!

I made my way back to San Francisco. I used some of the gold Mr. Wu had hidden in the jacket to start a fruit and vegetable store. After a while, my business began to do well. Now, I send my family enough money to live very well in China.

You may be wondering why I did not return to my homeland. Part of my heart stays in China. I carry photographs of my mother and father with me everywhere I go. Sometimes Chinese people are not treated fairly here. But the money I make here is better than the money I could make in China. Why did I immigrate to America? There are many challenges here. But there are many opportunities, too!

STOP AND CHECK

Why did Wai Ming stay in the U.S.?

Respond to Reading

Summarize

Use details from the story to summarize *The Promise of Gold Mountain*.

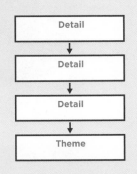

Detail
↓
Detail
↓
Detail
↓
Theme

Text Evidence

1. How do you know this is historical fiction? Genre

2. Why did Wai Ming go to America? Use details from the story to support your answer. Theme

3. Find the simile on page 10. What does it mean? Similes

4. Why did Wai Ming stay in America? Use important details from the story in your answer. Write About Reading

Compare Texts
Read about the California Gold Rush.

GOLD IN CALIFORNIA!

In 1848, something very exciting happened. A man named James Marshall found gold in a stream in California. At first, his boss, John Sutter, tried to keep it a secret. But the news spread like wildfire. Over time, it traveled all the way to the east coast of America. Newspapers splashed the news across their front pages.

Within months, a gold rush began. Thousands of people set off for California hoping to get rich. Some traveled west by wagon. They crossed plains, a desert, and mountains. Others traveled by boat. They sailed all the way around South America. Back then, both routes were dangerous and could take months.

MAIN ROUTES TO CALIFORNIA

San Francisco

N

KEY
— land route
— ocean route

This illustration shows men resting during their journey.

People from other countries also headed to California. Thousands came from Mexico and Chile. In 1852, more than 20,000 Chinese arrived hoping to find gold.

The people who came in search of gold changed California forever. In 1848, San Francisco was a small town of about 800. By 1852, it was a busy city. Over 250,000 people had flooded into California during the Gold Rush.

The modern city of San Francisco

Make Connections
How did the Gold Rush change California?
Essential Question

Which parts of Wai Ming's story could be true-to-life, or based on facts? Text to Text

Focus on Genre

Historical Fiction Historical fiction tells a story set in the past. The place where the story takes place could be real. There may be details in the story that come from history. However, the main characters are usually made up.

Read and Find *The Promise of Gold Mountain* is about a made-up person. However, the author studied real Chinese immigrants of the gold rush, so the story has some true-to-life details.

Your Turn

Choose a time in the past. Find out facts about this time. Write a story set in the past. Have your characters do things that people in that time would have done.